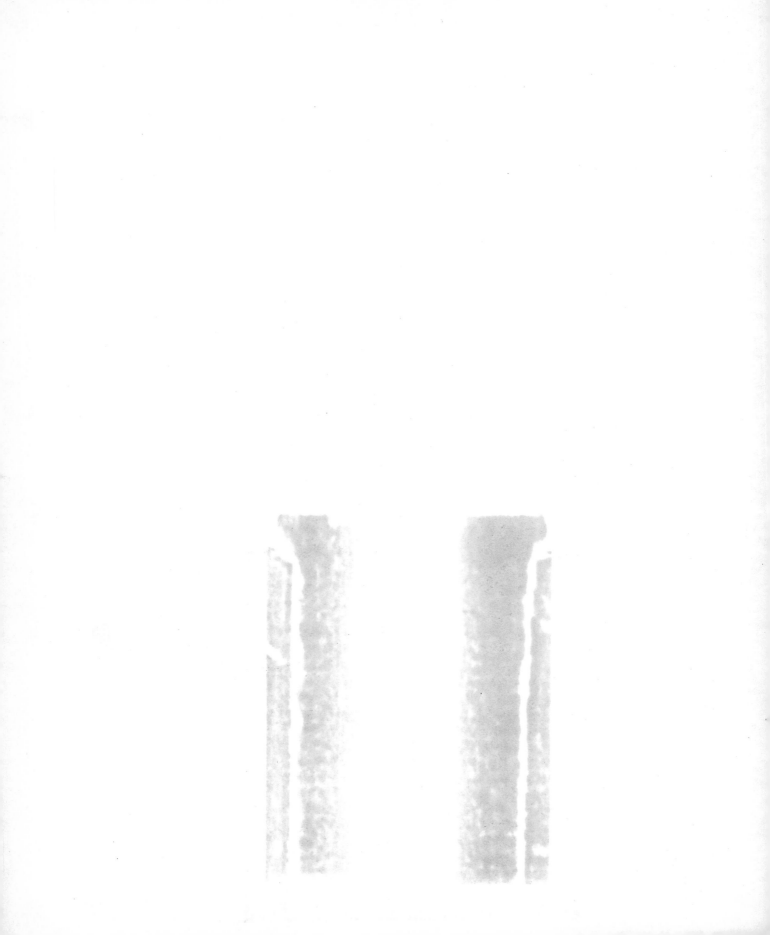

the Sleepover Cookbook

Hallie Warshaw

Photography by Julie Brown

Including healthy recipes by Diane Nepa M.N.S., R.D.

Sterling Publishing Co., Inc.
New York

THE SLEEPOVER COOKBOOK

Creative Director
Hallie Warshaw

Photographer
Julie Brown

Recipe Editor
Belena Raisin

Recipe Writers
Kris Bhat
Melanie Blitz
Rosemary Leas
Diane Nepa
Belena Raisin
Allison Stamey
Marsha Zander

Contributing Writer
Mark Shulman

Illustrators
Lisa Tabbush
Annie Galvin

Production Artists
Doug Popovich
Katrina Hendriks

Creative Director's Assistant/Prep Cook
Kris Bhat

Photographer's Assistant
Phyllis Christopher

Library of Congress Cataloging-in-Publication Data Available

10 9 8 7 6 5 4 3 2 1

Published by Sterling Publishing Company, Inc.
387 Park Avenue South, New York, NY 10016

© 2000 Hallie Warshaw
Photographs © 2000 Julie Brown

Created and produced by Orange Avenue, Inc.
275 Fifth Street, San Francisco, CA 94103, USA

Distributed in Canada by Sterling Publishing Co., Inc.
c/o Canadian Manda Group, One Atlantic Avenue, Suite 105
Toronto, Ontario, Canada M6K 3E7

Distributed in Great Britain and Europe by Chris Lloyd
463 Ashley Road, Parkstone, Poole, Dorset
BH14 0AX, England

Distributed in Australia by Capricorn Link (Australia) Pty Ltd.
P.O. Box 6651, Baulkham Hills, Business Centre
NSW 2153, Australia

Printed in China.

All rights reserved.

Sterling ISBN 0-8069-4497-8 Trade

THE SLEEPOVER COOKBOOK
Orange Avenue, Inc., San Francisco

THANK YOU... IT TAKES A LOT OF PEOPLE TO MAKE A BOOK!

Thanks goes to everyone who participated in the creation, execution and production of this book. We couldn't have done it without all of you!

CHILDREN MODELS

Justin Baker
Zane Baker
Maggie Belshaw
Surya Bhat
Katie Brooks
Dyantha Burton
Julia Burton
Nicholas Butler-Parker
Hannah Byers-Straus

Maya Cameron
Aaron Evans
Zoe Ho Seher
Jesse Jans-Neuberger
Ariel Krietzman
Nina Krietzman
Brian Ladd
Jessica Ladd
Kiger Lau

Bryan Locy
Katrina McGraw
Jenny McMillan
Lauren Moon
Lucia Oberste-Hufft
Erin Palmerston
Leslie Palmerston
Gabrielle Rodriguez-Fusco
Mario Rodriguez-Fusco

Christopher Scally
Tommy Scally
Sarah Seegal
Perry Shadwick
Emiko Shimabukuro
Andrew Slater
Benjamin Slater
Peter Sonnenberg
Emma Timboy-Pickering

And thanks to the parents and grown-ups for all the carpools, tips and support for the project!

RECIPES

Kris Bhat
Chicken Veggie Sticks
Cream Cheese and Ham Omelette
Real Shepherd's Pie

Melanie Blitz
Apple Pillows
Breakfast Pizza
Confetti Taco Salad
Honey Peanutty Dip
Peanut Butter and Jelly Cake
Rockin' Roll-ups

Rosemary Leas
Chewy Pretzel Letters
Hot Taco Dip

Diane Nepa
Banana Nut French Toast
Basket-of-Berries Smoothies
Cheesy Strawberry Cake
Fit-as-a-Fiddle Berry Pancakes
Gobble-Em-Up Turkey Burgers
Orange Chicken
No-Bake Blueberry Crumble

Belena Raisin
Banana Chocolate Drops
Bow-Tie Pasta Salad
Chocolate Polka Dot Muffins

Allison Stamey
Angel Fruit Cake
Chicken Pot Pie

Classic Chocolate Chip Cookies
Creative Crepes
Teatime with Scones
Favorite Chocolate Cake
Fish and Chips
Fundue
Ginger Ball Cookies
Guacamole and Tortilla Chips
Homemade Pizza
Peachy-Keen Cake
Spicy Spaghetti and Meatballs
Brownie Sundaes
Tasty Tart
What-a-Frittata

Marsha Zander
Sticky Popcorn Balls

PHOTOSHOOT HOMES

Thank you for volunteering your homes: Lili Byers and family, Ken and Kim High, Donna and Jack Krietzman, Kay Ladd and family, Sabina Lanier and family and Lynn Pearson and family.

In appreciation, a donation has been made to The Edgewood Center for Children and Families, San Francisco, an independent full-service residential and day program facility for emotionally disturbed, learning disabled children ages 5–14. The center promotes resiliency in children, strengthens families and supplements services in the community through many specialized programs.

SPECIAL THANKS

Kris Bhat, Phyllis Christopher, Belena Raisin, Doug Popovich and Mark Shulman.

Additional thanks: Charlie Nurnberg, Sheila Barry, Bob Warshaw, Elaine Warshaw, Ronnie Warshaw, Mark Warshaw, Fanye Stein, Marsha Zander, Diane Nepa, Lisa Tabbush, Annie Galvin, Katrina Hendriks, Beverley Sutherland, Robyn Brode, Paul Terry, Rosanne Roberts, Julie McCormack, Phred Huber, Michelle Antici, Candice Kollar, Ken High, Ellen Greenberg, Kay Ladd, Connie Johnson, Diane Green and The Renaissance Entrepreneurship Center, San Francisco.

WHAT'S COOKING?

1. STARTER SNACKS

Sticky Popcorn Balls	14
Fluffy S'mores	16
Classic Chocolate Chip Cookies	18
Ginger Ball Cookies	20
Banana Chocolate Drops	22
Apple Pillows	24
♥ No-Bake Blueberry Crumble	26

2. AWARD-WINNINER DINNERS

Chicken Pot Pie	34
Fish and Chips	36
Confetti Taco Salad	38
Spicy Spaghetti and Meatballs	40
Real Shepherd's Pie	42
Homemade Pizza	44
♥ Orange Chicken	46

3. SACKTIME SNACKS

Peanut Butter and Jelly Cake	54
Nutty Milkshakes	56
Guacamole and Tortilla Chips	58
Chewy Pretzel Letters	60
Honey Peanutty Dip	62
Hot Taco Dip	64
♥ Basket-of-Berries Smoothies	66

4. PAJAMA BREAKFASTS

Cream Cheese and Ham Omelette	74
What-a-Frittata	76
Chocolate Polka Dot Muffins	78
Banana Nut French Toast	80
Creative Crepes	82
Breakfast Pizza	84
♥ Fit-as-a-Fiddle Berry Pancakes	86

5. BRUNCH LUNCH & MUNCH

Tuna Meltdowns	94
Rockin' Roll-Ups	96
Bow-Tie Pasta Salad	98
Biscuit-Bite Pizza	100
Tasty Tart	102
Chicken Veggie Sticks	104
♥ Gobble-Em-Up Turkey Burgers	106

6. BIRTHDAY SURPRISES

Peachy-Keen Cake	114
Angel Fruit Cake	116
Fundue	118
Teatime with Scones	120
Brownie Sundaes	122
Favorite Chocolate Cake	124
♥ Cheesy Strawberry Cake	126

♥ Indicates healthy recipes

INTRODUCTION (FOR KIDS ONLY... THIS WILL BORE PARENTS.)

SO YOU GOT PERMISSION FOR SOME FRIENDS TO COME OVER? Good going—we knew you could do it. This is going to be fun. Now stick with this book and we'll show you how you can totally rule the kitchen.

FIRST THINGS FIRST. Recipes are more than just good advice. You should follow them closely. We know, we know...you think it's boring to follow directions. What happens if you don't? Well, your creation might taste like something the dog buried. It could be smelly (smoke) or loud (smoke detector) or really loud... like a grown-up yelling, "Who made this mess??? You kids go home!!!" Cleaning the kitchen alone is more boring than following recipes.

SECOND THINGS SECOND. You don't have to be on a sleepover to use this cookbook, but since "Sleepover" is in the title, we set up the menu that way. That's why we put dinners before brunch. If you want to eat midnight snacks at lunchtime or Orange Chicken for breakfast, that's your problem. We're here to help.

AND LASTLY... have fun but be smart. The original kitchen was a hole in the ground with a fire inside. The one in your house may have a microwave instead, but you can still get hurt. Don't forget that knives, stoves and potato peelers are, well, you know...

REMEMBER—IT'S ALL FUN AND GAMES UNTIL SOMEONE LOSES PERMISSION FOR THE NEXT SLEEPOVER.

COOKING STUFF

BAKING SHEET

CHOPPING BOARD

CAN OPENER

COLLANDER

DRY MEASURING CUPS
(for dry ingredients)

FRYING PAN

HAND MIXER

LIQUID MEASURING CUP
(for liquid ingredients)

MIXING BOWL

MEASURING SPOONS
(for dry and liquid ingredients)

MUFFIN TIN

POT HOLDERS

ROLLING PIN

ROUND CAKE PANS

SAUCEPAN

SIFTER

SLOTTED SPOON

SPATULA

SPRINGFORM PAN
(a cake pan where the bottom comes out)

SQUARE OR RECTANGULAR CAKE PAN

TUBE PAN

WIRE WHISK

WOODEN SPOON

COOK TALK

ROOM TEMPERATURE: Let the item sit out on the counter for about 30 minutes, or whenever it's the temperature of...you guessed it...the room.

SIFT TOGETHER: Using a sifter, mix the ingredients together until everything's evenly distributed.

MIX UNTIL JUST BLENDED: Mix until all the dry ingredients are just moistened. Do not overmix.

A PINCH: Like it sounds. Pretend you're a grandparent and the salt (or whatever) is your cheek.

CREAM: Sometimes goopy things like eggs, butter, margarine or milk need to be blended together. Take the back of a spoon and mush it all up until you get something like grainy cream cheese.

SET ASIDE: That's right, just leave it alone until the recipe lets you mess with it again.

KNEAD: Sounds like need...and you knead the dough more than it needs you. First shape the dough into a mound on a lightly floured bread board. Rest your fingers and palms lightly on the dough. Gently roll the dough away a little, then gently press down and backward with your palms. Give the dough a quarter turn and repeat the motion. Repeat until dough is smooth and elastic. Fight the urge to throw it around the kitchen.

SPRAY: Hold a can of vegetable cooking spray about a foot from your pan. Be careful how you point it. Lightly cover every part of the pan once.

READ THIS OR DIE!*

1. READ THE ENTIRE RECIPE BEFORE YOU BEGIN. FIND ALL THE INGREDIENTS AND UTENSILS FIRST, AND HAVE THEM READY TO USE.

Worst-Case Scenario:
You reach a critical point where you need 430 eggs. But you only have 317. You frantically call every chicken farmer in the phone book. Meanwhile, your meal grows very large and begins to attack you. You know that beating it back with a wooden spoon is the only way to save your life. But you forgot to get a wooden spoon, didn't you? The last thing you remember is the feel of angry, half-baked goo around your neck...

2. ALWAYS WASH YOUR HANDS BEFORE COOKING AND EATING.

Worst-Case Scenario:
Your neighborhood sits on a nuclear waste site. You keep touching your food with dirty hands. You catch poison germs the size of walnuts and you begin to glow in the dark...

3. ALWAYS USE POT HOLDERS WHEN HANDLING HOT DISHES, POTS AND PANS.

Worst-Case Scenario:
You burn off all your fingerprints. When the bandages are removed five months later, you can no longer get a driver's license. Maybe you'll find work as a scarecrow...

4. ALWAYS TIE YOUR HAIR BACK IF IT IS LONG.

Worst-Case Scenario:
Your hair catches fire. You rush to the sink. You are sucked down the drain by your hair and spend the rest of the school year in the sewer system...

5. ALWAYS CLEAN UP WHATEVER YOU USE.

Worst-Case Scenario:
You are banished from the kitchen forever, condemned to eat all your meals in the garage. Maybe when you learn to clean up your messes, you'll get a plate...

6. NEVER LEAVE ANY FOOD COOKING UNATTENDED IN THE OVEN OR ON THE STOVE.

Worst-Case Scenario:
The fire department puts your picture on its International List of Dummies, and the only clothes you have left are too small and smell like a burned refrigerator...

7. MAKE SURE AN ADULT IS NEARBY.

Worst-Case Scenario:
You get in trouble, but you live. You are grounded until the age of fifty-nine. No one ever comes over, and pretty soon everyone thinks your house is haunted. You promise to follow rules, but it's too late...

DON'T SAY WE DIDN'T WARN YOU!

* *Even in the worst-case scenarios, you will probably survive your cooking experiments. But there are so many ways you can hurt yourself in the kitchen. All we can say is **be careful...fingers don't grow back.***

COOKING KEY

TIMING

0-20 MINUTES

20-40 MINUTES

40-60 MINUTES

DIFFICULTY

SUPER SIMPLE
All play, no work.

EASY TREATS
A little effort goes a long way.

BRAIN FOOD
More preparation needed... but worth it!

FIRST YOUR FRIENDS COME OVER. They check out your new stuff. They play your games. And someone says, "What's there to eat around here?" And you say, "I've got the new Sleepover Cookbook," and they say, "But cookbooks taste lousy!" You roll your eyes and aim everyone into the kitchen before they eat your goldfish. If you want munchies that are like gourmet arts and crafts, you've come to the right place at the right time.

STARTER SNACKS

Sticky Popcorn Balls   14

Fluffy S'mores   16

Classic Chocolate Chip Cookies   18

Ginger Ball Cookies   20

Banana Chocolate Drops   22

Apple Pillows   24

♥ No-Bake Blueberry Crumble   26

STICKY POPCORN BALLS

Get Ready, Get Set...

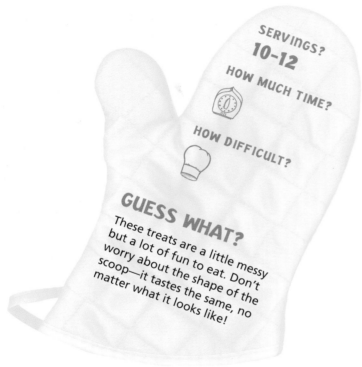

SERVINGS?
10-12

HOW MUCH TIME?

HOW DIFFICULT?

GUESS WHAT?

These treats are a little messy but a lot of fun to eat. Don't worry about the shape of the scoop—it tastes the same, no matter what it looks like!

Cook on the
Stove

Ingredients

16 cups popped popcorn

1 package (1 pound) favorite chocolate-coated candies

1 jar (16 ounces) dry roasted peanuts

8 ounces (1 stick) unsalted butter

½ cup corn oil

1 package (1 pound) marshmallows

Utensils & Tools

Liquid measuring cup

Dry measuring cups

Medium-size saucepan

Large mixing bowl

Wooden spoon

Baking sheet

Get Cooking!

1. Melt oil and butter in a saucepan over medium heat.

2. Add marshmallows and stir with a wooden spoon until completely melted.

3. In a large mixing bowl, pour the melted marshmallow mixture over popcorn and mix well to combine.

4. Add the chocolate-covered candies and peanuts.

5. Using a large spoon or your hands, scoop out 1-cup portions of the popcorn mixture onto a baking sheet.

6. Let the scoops cool slightly before serving.

FLUFFY S'MORES

Get Ready, Get Set...

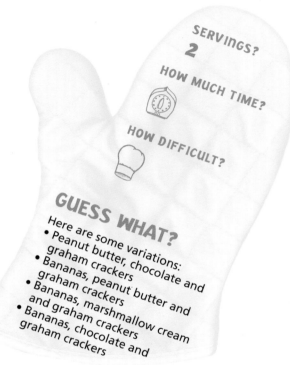

SERVINGS?
2

HOW MUCH TIME?

HOW DIFFICULT?

GUESS WHAT?
Here are some variations:
• Peanut butter, chocolate and graham crackers
• Bananas, peanut butter and graham crackers
• Bananas, marshmallow cream and graham crackers
• Bananas, chocolate and graham crackers

Ingredients

2 whole graham crackers
8 tablespoons marshmallow cream
1 bar (1½ ounces) plain chocolate, broken in half

Utensils & Tools

Measuring spoons
Spoon for spreading

Requires
no heating

Get Cooking!

1. Break one whole graham cracker in half.

2. Spread 2 tablespoons of the marshmallow cream on each half.

3. Place half of the chocolate bar between the two graham crackers.

4. Press the graham crackers together like a sandwich, with the chocolate in the center.

6. Repeat the process.

Get Ready, Get Set...

MAKES
24 cookies

HOW MUCH TIME?

HOW DIFFICULT?

GUESS WHAT?

It is important not to overmix the dough after you add the dry ingredients or the cookies will be tough.

Cook in the
Oven

Ingredients

1 egg

1 egg yolk

2¼ cups all-purpose flour

1 teaspoon salt

1 teaspoon baking soda

12 tablespoons (1½ sticks) unsalted butter, at room temperature

¾ cup light brown sugar

¾ cup granulated sugar

2½ teaspoons vanilla extract

1 package (12 ounces or 2 cups) semi-sweet chocolate chips

Utensils & Tools

Dry measuring cups

Measuring spoons

Small mixing bowl

Wire whisk

Medium mixing bowl

Sifter or strainer

Electric mixer

Wooden spoon

Baking sheet

Wire rack

Get Cooking!

1. Preheat oven to 350°.

2. In a small mixing bowl, whisk together the whole egg and egg yolk. Set aside.

3. In a medium mixing bowl, sift together the flour, salt and baking soda (dry ingredients). Set aside.

4. Using an electric mixer, cream together the butter and sugars until light and fluffy.

5. Add the eggs and vanilla extract and beat until smooth.

6. Slowly add the dry ingredients, mixing only until just blended.

7. With a wooden spoon, gently mix in the chocolate chips.

8. On a baking sheet, spoon tablespoon-size portions of the dough 3 inches apart.

9. Bake on the middle rack of the oven for 12–15 minutes.

10. Remove sheet from the oven with pot holders and cool cookies on a wire rack for 5 minutes.

11. Repeat process until all cookies have been baked.

GINGER BALL COOKIES

Get Ready, Get Set...

MAKES
36 cookies

HOW MUCH TIME?

HOW DIFFICULT?

GUESS WHAT?
It is important not to overmix the dough after you add the dry ingredients or the cookies will be tough.

Cook in the
Oven

Ingredients

1 whole egg

1 egg yolk

12 tablespoons (1½ sticks) unsalted butter, at room temperature

2 cups granulated sugar

⅓ cup unsulphured molasses

2¼ cups all-purpose flour

1½ teaspoons salt

2 teaspoons baking soda

1 tablespoon ground ginger

1½ teaspoons ground cinnamon

½ teaspoon ground cloves

Utensils & Tools

Liquid measuring cup

Dry measuring cups

Measuring spoons

2 small mixing bowls

Wire whisk

Medium mixing bowl

Sifter or strainer

Electric mixer

Baking sheet

Wire rack

Get Cooking!

1. Preheat oven to 375°.

2. In a small mixing bowl, whisk together the egg and egg yolk. Set aside.

3. In a medium mixing bowl, sift together the flour, salt, baking soda, ginger, cinnamon and cloves (dry ingredients). Set aside.

4. Using an electric mixer, cream together the butter and 1 cup of sugar until light and fluffy.

5. Add eggs and molasses and mix until smooth. Add the dry ingredients, mixing until just blended.

6. Spoon tablespoon-size portions of dough into your hand and shape into balls.

7. In a small mixing bowl, put remaining 1 cup of sugar.

8. Roll each ball in the sugar and place on a baking sheet 3 inches apart.

9. Flatten each ball with a fork that has been dipped in the sugar to make a decorative top.

10. Bake on the middle rack of the oven for 6–7 minutes.

11. Remove baking sheet from oven with pot holders and cool cookies on a wire rack for 5 minutes.

12. Repeat process until all cookies have been baked.

BANANA CHOCOLATE DROPS

Get Ready, Get Set...

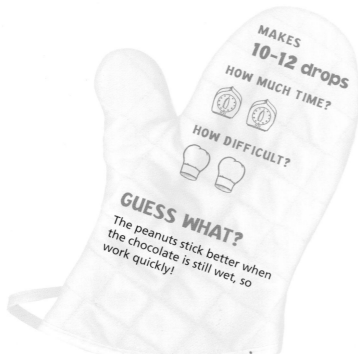

MAKES
10-12 drops

HOW MUCH TIME?

HOW DIFFICULT?

GUESS WHAT?
The peanuts stick better when the chocolate is still wet, so work quickly!

Ingredients

1 package (12 ounces) semi-sweet chocolate chips

1 cup chopped peanuts

2 bananas, cut into 1-inch pieces

Utensils & Tools

Small saucepan

Stainless steel bowl

Baking sheet or large plate

Wax paper or aluminum foil

Small mixing bowl

Wooden spoon

Toothpicks

Cook on the
Stove

Get Cooking!

1. In a small saucepan, bring 1 cup of water to a boil. Place the chocolate chips in a stainless steel bowl and set it on top of the saucepan.

2. Turn the burner off and allow the chocolate to melt over the steaming water.

3. While the chocolate is melting, select a baking sheet or large plate that fits into your freezer. Line it with wax paper or aluminum foil.

4. Place the peanuts in a small mixing bowl or on a plate. Set aside.

5. Stir the chocolate with a wooden spoon until it is smooth and completely melted.

6. Skewer each piece of banana with a toothpick and dip into the chocolate.

7. Roll the banana in the chocolate until completely coated.

8. Using the toothpick as a handle, roll the banana in the peanuts.

9. Place the coated banana on the baking sheet or plate.

10. Repeat process until all banana pieces have been dipped.

11. Freeze bananas for 1 hour before serving.

APPLE PILLOWS

Get Ready, Get Set...

MAKES
10 pillows

HOW MUCH TIME?

HOW DIFFICULT?

GUESS WHAT?
Let the pillows cool slightly before eating—they are hot inside!

Ingredients

1 package (8 ounces) refrigerated crescent rolls

1 small apple, peeled and finely chopped

½ cup raisins

¼ cup chopped pecans

1 tablespoon light brown sugar

3 tablespoons granulated sugar

Milk for brushing

Cinnamon for sprinkling

Granulated sugar for sprinkling

Vegetable cooking spray

Utensils & Tools

Dry measuring cups

Measuring spoons

Baking sheet

Medium mixing bowl

Pastry brush

Wire rack

Cook in the
Oven

Get Cooking!

1. Preheat oven to 350°.

2. Separate crescent rolls into individual triangles and arrange on a lightly greased baking sheet.

3. In a medium mixing bowl, mix together the apple, raisins, pecans, brown sugar and cinnamon.

4. Place teaspoon-size portions of the apple mixture onto the center of each triangle.

5. Roll up the dough into a crescent shape.

6. Lightly brush the tops of the crescents with milk and sprinkle with cinnamon and sugar.

7. Bake on the middle rack of the oven for 25 minutes or until golden brown.

8. Remove sheet from the oven with pot holders and cool on a wire rack.

NO-BAKE BLUEBERRY CRUMBLE

Get Ready, Get Set...

SERVINGS?
8-10

HOW MUCH TIME?

HOW DIFFICULT?

GUESS WHAT?
♥ *Why is this good for you?*
Blueberries are high in vitamin C, potassium and fiber.
Serve crumble with vanilla ice cream or frozen yogurt.

Ingredients

1 cup nutlike cereal nuggets

2 bananas, sliced into thirds lengthwise

⅓ cup unsweetened frozen apple juice concentrate, thawed

2 tablespoons cornstarch

½ cup cold water

4 cups unsweetened frozen blueberries, thawed, or 4 cups fresh blueberries

1 teaspoon vanilla extract

Utensils & Tools

Liquid measuring cup

Dry measuring cups

Measuring spoons

10-inch pie pan

Small mixing bowl

Wire whisk

Medium saucepan

Cook on the
Stove

Get Cooking!

1. Layer the bottom of a 10-inch pie pan with the cereal and top with the bananas. Set aside.

2. In a small mixing bowl, combine the cornstarch and water and whisk until smooth.

3. In a medium saucepan over medium heat, bring the apple juice concentrate to a boil. Add the cornstarch and water mixture and stir continuously until the apple juice thickens to the consistency of a thick syrup.

4. Reduce the heat to low and add the blueberries and vanilla extract to the saucepan. Gently stir until the glaze completely coats the blueberries.

5. Remove the saucepan from the heat using pot holders.

6. Pour the fruit mixture over the bananas and cereal.

7. Cool to room temperature before serving.

27

BACK IN THE WILD WEST,

the cook in the wagon train would use a dinner bell to call the hungry pioneers to dinner. They'd pull off their hats and go sit down, covered in dust. Holding a knife in one hand and a fork in the other, they'd growl, "What's fer grub?" Sound like fun? Well, not tonight, pal. It's your turn to cook. If the pioneers had Homemade Pizza and Confetti Taco Salad, the West might have been less wild.

AWARD WINNER DINNERS

Chicken Pot Pie 34

Fish and Chips 36

Confetti Taco Salad 38

Spicy Spaghetti and Meatballs 40

Real Shepherd's Pie 42

Homemade Pizza 44

♥ Orange Chicken 46

CHICKEN POT PIE

Get Ready, Get Set...

SERVINGS?
6-8

HOW MUCH TIME?

HOW DIFFICULT?

GUESS WHAT?
If the two pie dough layers are not staying together properly, brush a little water or a beaten egg between them.

Ingredients

1 package ready-made pie dough (2 layers in a package)

2–3 tablespoons vegetable oil

1 large yellow onion, diced

2 carrots, sliced into $\frac{1}{4}$-inch thick pieces

1 cup fresh or frozen peas

1 cup fresh or frozen corn

2 cups cooked chicken, diced

1 can cream of mushroom soup

1 tablespoon milk

Pinch of salt, pinch of pepper

Utensils & Tools

Dry measuring cups

Measuring spoons

9-inch pie pan

Medium-size frying pan

Cook on the
Stove

Cook in the
Oven

Get Cooking!

1. Preheat oven to 375°.

2. Line a 9-inch pie pan with one layer of the pie dough. Gently press the dough on the bottom and up the sides of the pan to form a crust.

3. In a medium-size frying pan over medium-high heat, cook the chopped onions and carrots for 5–7 minutes. Add peas and corn. Continue to cook 3–4 minutes. Remove from heat. Add the diced chicken pieces.

4. Stir in the cream of mushroom soup and the milk.

5. Add salt and pepper.

6. Pour the entire mixture into the pie pan.

7. Cover the pie pan with a top layer of pie dough. Join the two layers by crimping them together with your fingers. Cut or poke some small holes in the top of the dough to allow steam to escape.

8. Bake on the middle rack of the oven for 35–40 minutes or until the crust is golden brown.

9. Remove pie from the oven using pot holders and set aside to cool for 5–10 minutes before serving.

Get Ready, Get Set...

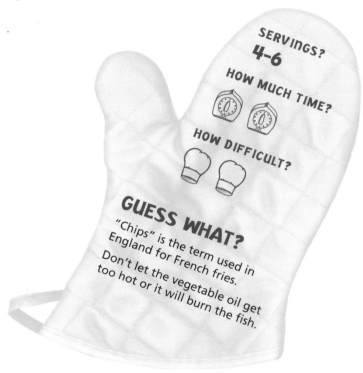

SERVINGS?
4-6

HOW MUCH TIME?

HOW DIFFICULT?

GUESS WHAT?

"Chips" is the term used in England for French fries.

Don't let the vegetable oil get too hot or it will burn the fish.

Cook on the Stove

Cook in the Oven

Ingredients

For the chips

3 russet or Idaho potatoes, cut into ½-inch by 3-inch strips

Vegetable oil for brushing

Salt for sprinkling

For the fish

1 cup all-purpose flour

1 teaspoon salt

1 teaspoon black pepper

2 cups buttermilk

3 tablespoons vegetable oil

1½ pounds cod or halibut filets, cut into ½-inch by 3-inch strips

1 jar tartar sauce

Utensils & Tools

Baking sheet

Liquid measuring cup

Dry measuring cups

Measuring spoons

Medium-size frying pan

Slotted spatula

Shallow bowl or baking dish

Paper towels

Get Cooking!

For the chips

1. Arrange potatoes on a baking sheet.

2. Lightly brush potatoes with vegetable oil.

3. Bake on the middle rack of the oven for **20–25** minutes or until well browned.

4. Remove baking sheet from oven.

5. Sprinkle potatoes with salt.

For the fish

1. In a shallow bowl or baking dish, combine the flour, salt and pepper.

2. In another shallow bowl or baking dish, pour in the buttermilk.

3. Dip each piece of fish into the buttermilk and then into the flour mixture, coating both sides.

4. Pour vegetable oil into a medium-size frying pan over medium heat.

5. Carefully place the fish, a few pieces at a time, into the pan. Cook on each side for 5 minutes or until golden brown.

5. Using a slotted spatula, carefully remove the fish from the hot oil and drain on paper towels.

Serve with tartar sauce.

CONFETTI TACO SALAD

Get Ready, Get Set...

SERVINGS?
4-6

HOW MUCH TIME?

HOW DIFFICULT?

GUESS WHAT?
If you don't like ground beef, substitute 3 cups of shredded cooked turkey or chicken.

Ingredients

1 pound ground beef

1 envelope (1¼ ounces) taco seasoning mix

1 can (16 ounces) kidney beans, drained

1 large tomato, chopped

1 head lettuce, torn into small pieces

2 cups shredded cheddar cheese

1 big package corn chips

1 jar favorite salad dressing

Utensils & Tools

Dry measuring cups

Medium-size frying pan

Slotted spoon

Paper towels

Cook on the
Stove

Get Cooking!

1. In a medium-size frying pan, cook the beef until browned and crumbled.

2. Using a slotted spoon, remove the beef from the pan and drain on paper towels.

3. In a large mixing bowl, combine the beef and taco seasoning.

4. Add the beans, tomatoes, lettuce, cheese and corn chips.

5. Toss the entire mixture together.

Serve the salad in individual bowls with your favorite salad dressing.

Get Ready, Get Set...

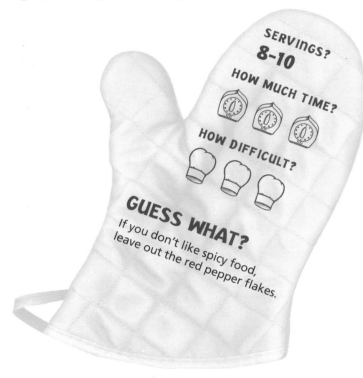

SERVINGS?
8-10

HOW MUCH TIME?

HOW DIFFICULT?

GUESS WHAT?
If you don't like spicy food, leave out the red pepper flakes.

Ingredients

For the meatballs

¾ pound ground beef

¾ pound ground pork

1 cup dry bread crumbs

1 tablespoon finely chopped garlic

½ teaspoon paprika

½ teaspoon cayenne pepper

1 teaspoon salt

½ teaspoon ground pepper

For the tomato sauce

3 tablespoons olive oil

½ cup finely chopped yellow onion

1 can (28 ounces) chopped tomatoes

½ teaspoon red pepper flakes

1½ teaspoons salt

1 pound dried spaghetti, cooked and drained according to package instructions

Utensils & Tools

Dry measuring cups	Baking sheet
Measuring spoons	Aluminum foil
Large mixing bowl	Large frying pan
Wooden spoon	Large serving bowl

Cook on the
Stove

Cook in the
Oven

Get Cooking!

For the meatballs

1. Preheat oven to 375°.

2. In a large mixing bowl, add all meatball ingredients and mix together with a strong wooden spoon or your hands.

3. Spoon 2 tablespoon-size portions into your hands and roll into balls.

4. Place meatballs (approximately 30) on a baking sheet.

5. Bake on the middle rack of the oven for 10–12 minutes or until meatballs are completely cooked.

6. Remove the sheet from the oven using pot holders.

7. Cover the meatballs with aluminum foil. Set aside.

For the tomato sauce

1. In a large frying pan over medium heat, add the olive oil.

2. Cook the onions in the oil for 3–4 minutes.

3. Add the tomatoes and cook for 12–15 minutes.

4. Add salt and red pepper flakes.

In a serving bowl, combine the pasta, tomato sauce and meatballs.

REAL SHEPHERD'S PIE

Get Ready, Get Set...

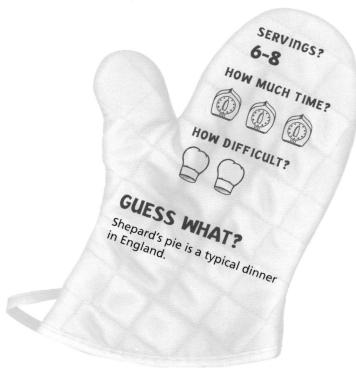

SERVINGS?
6-8

HOW MUCH TIME?

HOW DIFFICULT?

GUESS WHAT?
Shepard's pie is a typical dinner in England.

Cook on the
Stove

Cook in the
Oven

Ingredients

For the crust

1 package ready-made pie dough
(2 layers in a package)

For the filling

½ pound ground beef

½ cup diced yellow onion

1 cup sliced mushrooms

2 medium carrots, peeled and sliced
into ¼-inch thick pieces

For the topping

2 russet or Idaho potatoes, peeled and sliced
into ½-inch thick pieces

⅓ cup milk

1 tablespoon unsalted butter

¼ teaspoon salt

Utensils & Tools

Liquid measuring cup

Dry measuring cups

Measuring spoons

9-inch pie pan

Medium-size frying pan

Large pot

Medium mixing bowl

Potato masher or large wooden spoon

Get Cooking!

1. Preheat oven to 400°.

2. Line a 9-inch pie pan with one layer of the pie dough. Gently press the dough on the bottom and up the sides of the pan to form a crust.

3. Precook the crust on the middle rack of the oven for 20 minutes.

4. In a medium-size frying pan over medium heat, cook the beef until browned and crumbled.

5. Add the onions, mushrooms and carrots to the pan and cook for 5 minutes.

6. Bring a large pot of water to a boil and cook the potatoes until soft, about 5 minutes.

7. In a medium mixing bowl, using a potato masher or large wooden spoon, mash together the cooked potatoes, milk, butter and salt.

8. Spoon the beef and vegetables into the bottom of the precooked pie crust.

9. Layer the mashed potatoes on top of the beef and vegetables.

10. Bake the pie on the middle rack of the oven for 15 minutes or until the top of the potatoes is lightly browned.

11. Remove from oven using pot holders and cool for 5–10 minutes before serving.

HOMEMADE PIZZA

Get Ready, Get Set...

MAKES
4 pizzas

HOW MUCH TIME?

HOW DIFFICULT?

GUESS WHAT?

Use any other favorite toppings to create a unique pizza ...try sliced ham and pineapple for a Hawaiian-style pizza.

Cook in the
Oven

Ingredients

For the dough

4 cups all-purpose flour

$\frac{1}{2}$ cup cornmeal

2 tablespoons active dry yeast

$\frac{1}{2}$ teaspoon sugar

$1\frac{1}{2}$ tablespoons salt

2 tablespoons olive oil

$\frac{3}{4}$ cup water

Vegetable cooking spray

For the sauce

2 cups tomato sauce

4 teaspoons olive oil

2 teaspoons salt

1 teaspoon black pepper

For the toppings

4 cups shredded mozzarella cheese

$\frac{1}{2}$ cup grated Parmesan cheese

$\frac{1}{2}$ cup roughly chopped fresh basil

Utensils & Tools

Liquid measuring cup

Dry measuring cups

Measuring spoons

Large mixing bowl

Dry kitchen towel

Small mixing bowl

Rolling pin

Baking sheet

Get Cooking!

1. In a large mixing bowl, combine the flour and cornmeal. Make a well in the center and add the yeast, sugar, salt, oil and water.

2. Using your hands, mix together for approximately 5 minutes or until the dough feels smooth. If the dough feels too sticky, add a little more flour. If the dough feels too dry, add a little more water.

3. Cover the dough with a dry kitchen towel and let it rise in a warm area of the kitchen for 1 to 1½ hours or until it has doubled in size.

4. While the dough is rising, combine all pizza sauce ingredients in a small mixing bowl. Set aside.

5. Preheat oven to 500°.

6. Turn the dough out onto a lightly floured flat kitchen counter and cut into 4 equal portions.

7. Using a rolling pin, flatten each piece of dough into a 10-inch circle. Dust the dough with flour so it does not stick to the counter or the rolling pin. Place each circle on a lightly sprayed baking sheet.

8. Divide the pizza sauce, cheeses and basil evenly between the 4 pizzas.

9. Bake on the middle rack of the oven for 7 minutes or until the dough is golden brown and the cheese is bubbly.

10. Remove from the oven using pot holders and serve while warm.

ORANGE CHICKEN

Get Ready, Get Set...

SERVINGS?
4

HOW MUCH TIME?

HOW DIFFICULT?

GUESS WHAT?

♥ Why is this good for you? Skinless chicken breasts are high in protein and low in fat.

Ingredients

4 chicken breasts, boneless and skinless

½ cup orange jam, no sugar added

1 tablespoon low-sodium soy sauce

1 tablespoon rice vinegar

2 teaspoons honey Dijon mustard

2 cloves fresh garlic, finely chopped

Utensils & Tools

Dry measuring cups

Measuring spoons

Ovenproof baking dish

Small mixing bowl

Cook in the
Oven

Get Cooking!

1. Preheat oven to 400°.

2. Place chicken breasts in a baking dish.

3. In a small mixing bowl, mix together the jam, soy sauce, rice vinegar, mustard and garlic.

4. Pour the mixture evenly over the chicken breasts. Bake on the middle rack of the oven for 20–25 minutes or until chicken is white all the way through.

5. Remove baking dish from oven using pot holders.

Serve chicken with pasta or rice.

"OKAY, KIDS. BRUSH YOUR TEETH. Hop under the covers. Turn out the lights. Good night." Yeah, right. Everyone knows that slumber parties begin at bedtime. And everyone knows that kids make less noise with food in their mouths. Remind a grown-up about this and you'll be in the kitchen making Chewy Pretzel Letters and other treats all night long.

SACKTIME
SNACKS

Peanut Butter and Jelly Cake 54

Nutty Milkshakes 56

Guacamole and Tortilla Chips 58

Chewy Pretzel Letters 60

Honey Peanutty Dip 62

Hot Taco Dip 64

♥ Basket-of-Berries Smoothies 66

PEANUT BUTTER AND JELLY CAKE

Get Ready, Get Set...

SERVINGS?
8-10

HOW MUCH TIME?

HOW DIFFICULT?

GUESS WHAT?
It is easier to mix the frosting when the butter and peanut butter are at room temperature.

Requires
no heating

Ingredients

1 store-bought pound cake

½ cup favorite fruit jelly

For the frosting

¼ cup creamy peanut butter

3 tablespoons unsalted butter or margarine, at room temperature

1 teaspoon vanilla extract

2 cups powdered sugar, sifted

¼ cup milk

Utensils & Tools

Liquid measuring cup

Dry measuring cups

Measuring spoons

Electric mixer

Get Cooking!

1. Cut the pound cake in half in the middle.

2. Spread the jelly evenly on the cut sides of the cake.

3. Sandwich the two sides back together. Set aside.

4. Using an electric mixer, cream together the peanut butter and butter until light and fluffy.

5. Add the vanilla and continue beating.

6. Add the sugar and milk, a little at a time, and continue beating until smooth and spreadable.

7. Cover the entire cake with the peanut butter frosting.

Get Ready, Get Set...

SERVINGS?
1-2

HOW MUCH TIME?

HOW DIFFICULT?

GUESS WHAT?
To make this an extra-special treat, top each milkshake with whipped cream and some chocolate sprinkles!

Ingredients

2 bananas
½ cup milk
½ cup vanilla ice cream or frozen yogurt
½ cup smooth peanut butter

Utensils & Tools

Liquid measuring cup
Dry measuring cups
Blender

Requires
No heating

Get Cooking!

1. Put ingredients into a blender, one at a time.

2. Blend all ingredients until smooth.

Serve in chilled glasses.

Variations:

Try using chocolate milk, chocolate ice cream or strawberries.

Get Ready, Get Set...

SERVINGS?
8

HOW MUCH TIME?

HOW DIFFICULT?

GUESS WHAT?
Did you know that avocado is a fruit, not a vegetable?

Ingredients

For the tortilla chips
12 corn tortillas
Salt for sprinkling

For the guacamole
2 ripe avocados
$\frac{1}{2}$ cup store-bought salsa
$\frac{1}{4}$ cup sour cream
1 tablespoon lemon juice
$\frac{3}{4}$ teaspoon salt

Utensils & Tools

Liquid measuring cup
Measuring spoons
Baking sheet
Medium mixing bowl
Large fork

Cook in the
Oven

Get Cooking!

1. Preheat oven to 400°.

2. Cut each tortilla into 8 equal wedges and arrange in a single layer on a baking sheet. Sprinkle with salt.

3. Bake on the middle rack of the oven for 5 minutes or until crispy.

4. Remove chips from the oven with pot holders and set aside to cool.

5. Cut the avocados in half lengthwise and throw away pits.

6. Scoop the avocado away from the skin with a spoon and into a medium mixing bowl.

7. Mash the avocados with a large fork.

8. Add the remaining guacamole ingredients and mix until thoroughly combined.

Serve tortilla chips and guacamole together.

Get Ready, Get Set...

SERVINGS?

6

HOW MUCH TIME?

HOW DIFFICULT?

GUESS WHAT?

To make these a sweet treat, sprinkle with cinnamon and sugar instead of coarse salt.

Cook in the
Oven

Ingredients

1½ cups warm water

1 package (¼ ounce or **2** teaspoons) active dry yeast

½ teaspoon granulated sugar

Pinch of salt

4½ cups all-purpose flour

1 egg for brushing

Coarse salt for sprinkling

Vegetable cooking spray

Utensils & Tools

Liquid measuring cup

Dry measuring cups

Measuring spoons

Large mixing bowl

Aluminum foil

Baking sheet

Pastry brush

Wire rack

Get Cooking!

1. In a large mixing bowl, combine warm water, yeast, sugar and a pinch of salt. Add 2 cups of flour to the bowl and mix dough until smooth.

2. Add 2 additional cups of flour, working the last cup in with your hands.

3. If the dough is too sticky, add a little more flour— but not more than 1 cup.

4. Turn the dough out onto a lightly floured work surface and knead for 10 minutes.

5. Place dough in a lightly sprayed large mixing bowl, turning over to coat all sides with oil. Cover the bowl with aluminum foil and refrigerate for 2 hours.

6. Preheat oven to 475°.

7. Take the bowl out of the refrigerator and punch dough down to break all the air bubbles.

8. Divide dough into 6 equal pieces. Roll each piece into a rope 10–12 inches long.

9. Shape the dough into one of your initials or another creative design.

10. Place the pretzels on a lightly greased baking sheet 1 inch apart.

11. In a small bowl, whisk together egg and 1 tablespoon of water. Using a pastry brush, spread a thin coat of the egg mixture on each pretzel and sprinkle with salt.

12. Bake on the middle rack of the oven for 12–15 minutes or until golden brown.

13. Remove from the oven using pot holders and allow to cool slightly before serving.

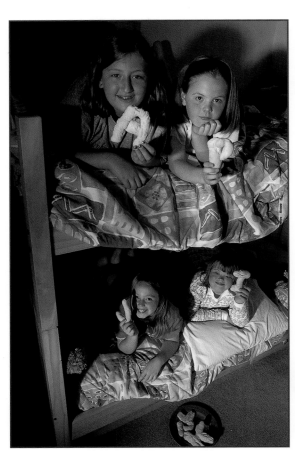

HONEY PEANUTTY DIP

Get Ready, Get Set...

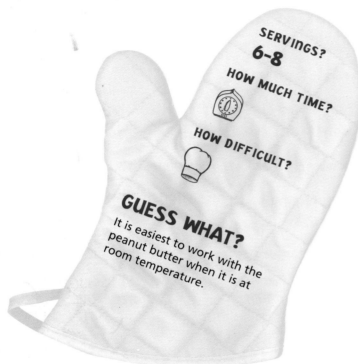

SERVINGS?
6-8

HOW MUCH TIME?

HOW DIFFICULT?

GUESS WHAT?
It is easiest to work with the peanut butter when it is at room temperature.

Requires
No heating

Ingredients

For the dip

1 cup crunchy peanut butter

1/3 cup honey

2/3 cup evaporated milk

3/4 cup raisins

1/4 teaspoon cinnamon

2 tablespoons slivered almonds

For the dippers

Apple slices

Banana chunks

Pretzels

Celery sticks

Carrot sticks

Utensils & Tools

Liquid measuring cup

Dry measuring cups

Measuring spoons

Medium mixing bowl

Wooden spoon

Get Cooking!

1. In a medium mixing bowl, combine the peanut butter, honey and milk.

2. Stir until smooth.

3. Add the raisins and cinnamon and stir until combined.

4. Place the dip into a serving dish and sprinkle with slivered almonds.

Serve dip with apple slices, banana chunks, pretzels, celery sticks and carrot sticks.

HOT TACO DIP

Get Ready, Get Set...

SERVINGS?
6-8

HOW MUCH TIME?

HOW DIFFICULT?

GUESS WHAT?
Wait a few minutes before dipping chips into dip. Hot cheese can burn your mouth! Have plenty of paper napkins on hand!

Ingredients

1 package (8 ounces) cream cheese

1 can (10½ ounces) chili without beans

1 can (4 ounces or ¼ cup) mild diced green chili peppers

1 cup shredded cheddar cheese

½ cup diced onion

1 bag tortilla chips

Utensils & Tools

Dry measuring cups

9-inch pie pan

Can opener

Cook in the
Oven

Get Cooking!

1. Preheat oven to 400°.

2. Spread the cream cheese over the bottom of a 9-inch pie pan.

3. Spread chili over the cream cheese. Sprinkle onion on top of the chili.

4. Drain liquid from the diced green chili peppers and spread them on top of the onion layer.

5. Sprinkle the top with cheddar cheese.

6. Bake on the middle rack of the oven for 15 minutes or until the cheese is bubbly.

7. Remove pan from the oven with pot holders and set aside to cool slightly.

Serve with tortilla chips.

BASKET-OF-BERRIES SMOOTHIES

Get Ready, Get Set...

SERVINGS?
1-2

HOW MUCH TIME?

HOW DIFFICULT?

GUESS WHAT?
♥ *Why is this good for you? Full of calcium, vitamin C, potassium and fiber, you can enjoy this high-energy treat any time of the day or night.*

Ingredients

1 cup milk, nonfat or low fat

½ cup nonfat frozen yogurt or fruit sherbet

1 banana

½ cup fresh or frozen berries

Utensils & Tools

Liquid measuring cup

Dry measuring cups

Blender

Bowl

Requires
no heating

Get Cooking!

1. Put ingredients into a blender, one at a time.

2. Blend all ingredients until smooth.

Serve in chilled glasses.

Variations:

Use any kind of berries or combination of berries.

To make a healthier smoothie, substitute soy milk for regular milk.

SLUMBER PARTY-ERS WAKE UP HUNGRY. It's a fact of science. They also wake up early. Here's a bunch of breakfast ideas that are so good and so easy to make, you'll never eat cereal again. Well, at least not the boring stuff. What's that, you say? You want to make Breakfast Pizza and Creative Crepes? This book changes all the rules. Except the one that says, "Don't cook without an adult. An awake adult." How they wake up is up to you.

PAJAMA BREAKFASTS

Cream Cheese and Ham Omelette 74

What-a-Frittata 76

Chocolate Polka Dot Muffins 78

Banana Nut French Toast 80

Creative Crepes 82

Breakfast Pizza 84

❤ Fit-as-a-Fiddle Berry Pancakes 86

Get Ready, Get Set...

SERVINGS?
2

HOW MUCH TIME?

HOW DIFFICULT?

GUESS WHAT?

This omelette works better if it is not turned over; the cream cheese makes it too messy! Repeat this recipe as many times as needed to feed all your friends!

Ingredients

2 eggs

⅓ cup milk

½ cup diced ham

1 tablespoon unsalted butter

1 package (8 ounces) cream cheese

Utensils & Tools

Liquid measuring cup

Dry measuring cups

Measuring spoons

Small mixing bowl

Wire whisk

Small frying pan with lid

Cook on the
Stove

Get Cooking!

1. In a small bowl, whisk together the eggs and milk.

2. Add ham to the bowl and stir to combine.

3. In a small frying pan over medium heat, melt the butter.

4. Pour the egg and ham mixture into the center of the frying pan.

5. Roll up the cream cheese into small balls and dot them on the surface of the omelette.

6. Cover the omelette with a lid and cook until the top has completely set.

7. Carefully transfer omelette to a serving plate.

Get Ready, Get Set...

SERVINGS?
8-10

HOW MUCH TIME?

HOW DIFFICULT?

GUESS WHAT?

Don't let the frittata stay in the oven too long or the eggs will not be moist.

To make a complete meal, serve with some roasted or hash brown potatoes and toast.

Ingredients

8 eggs

½ cup heavy cream

1½ cups corn kernels, canned or frozen and thawed

1 cup store-bought chunky salsa

1 cup shredded jack cheese

1 teaspoon salt

1 tablespoon unsalted butter

Utensils & Tools

Liquid measuring cup

Dry measuring cups

Measuring spoons

Large mixing bowl

Wire whisk

Large ovenproof frying pan with lid

Cook on the
Stove

Cook in the
Oven

Get Cooking!

1. Preheat oven to 400°.

2. In a large mixing bowl, whisk together the eggs, cream, corn, salsa, cheese and salt.

3. In a large ovenproof frying pan* over medium-high heat, melt the butter. Pour the egg mixture into the center of the frying pan and cover. Reduce heat to low. Cook frittata until eggs are almost set, about 8 minutes.

4. Place the pan, uncovered, on the middle rack for about 3 minutes, until the top is just beginning to lightly brown.

5. Remove pan from oven using pot holders.

6. Carefully slide the frittata out of the pan and onto a serving plate.

7. Cut into 8 equal wedges and serve immediately.

* Make sure the handle of the pan is not plastic or some other material that could melt in the oven.

Get Ready, Get Set...

MAKES
12 muffins

HOW MUCH TIME?

HOW DIFFICULT?

GUESS WHAT?
It is important not to overmix the batter or the muffins will be tough and chewy.

Cook in the
Oven

Ingredients

2 cups all-purpose flour

1³/₄ teaspoons baking powder

¹/₂ teaspoon baking soda

³/₄ cup granulated sugar

¹/₂ teaspoon salt

1 egg

1 cup buttermilk

4 tablespoons (¹/₂ stick) unsalted butter, melted and cooled

¹/₂ cup semi-sweet chocolate chips

Utensils & Tools

Liquid measuring cup

Dry measuring cups

Measuring spoons

Large mixing bowl

Sifter or strainer

Wire whisk

Small mixing bowl

Muffin pan

Muffin pan cups

Get Cooking!

1. Preheat oven to 400°.

2. In a large mixing bowl, sift together the flour, baking powder, baking soda, sugar and salt (dry ingredients).

3. Add the chocolate chips and stir to combine.

4. Form a well in the middle of the dry ingredients.

5. In a small mixing bowl, whisk together the egg, buttermilk and butter.

6. Pour the egg mixture into the well of the dry ingredients and mix until just blended.

7. Line a muffin pan with muffin pan cups.

8. Spoon batter into prepared muffin pan cups.

9. Bake on the middle rack of the oven for 20 minutes.

10. Remove from the oven using pot holders and remove muffins from tin to cool.

BANANA NUT FRENCH TOAST

Get Ready, Get Set...

SERVINGS?
2

HOW MUCH TIME?

HOW DIFFICULT?

GUESS WHAT?

♥ Why is this good for you? Whole-wheat bread or raisin bread provides more fiber, vitamins and minerals than enriched white bread.

Cook on the
Stove

Ingredients

2 eggs

½ cup nonfat milk

1 teaspoon cinnamon

4 slices whole-wheat or cinnamon raisin bread, cut in half diagonally

2 bananas, chopped into small pieces

¼ cup chopped nuts

Maple syrup or applesauce

Vegetable cooking spray

Utensils & Tools

Liquid measuring cup

Dry measuring cups

Measuring spoons

Shallow bowl

Wire whisk

Wooden spoon

Large frying pan

Spatula

Get Cooking!

1. In a medium mixing bowl, whisk the eggs until foamy.

2. Add the milk and cinnamon and stir to combine.

3. Spread the chopped nuts onto a plate. Set aside.

4. Lightly coat a large frying pan with cooking spray and place over medium heat.

5. Dip each bread slice in the wet ingredients, coating both sides. Coat each side with the chopped nuts.

6. Place bread in the frying pan. Cook until underside is golden brown. Gently flip the bread over. Firmly place banana pieces on top of each piece of bread and continue cooking until other side is golden brown.

Serve with a drizzle of maple syrup or applesauce.

Get Ready, Get Set...

SERVINGS?
14–16

HOW MUCH TIME?

HOW DIFFICULT?

GUESS WHAT?

"Crepe" is the French word for a thin pancake.

Don't worry if your first crepe doesn't come out perfectly—even professional chefs can ruin the first few crepes in a batch!

Ingredients

1²/₃ cups all-purpose flour

1 teaspoon salt

2¹/₃ cups milk

2 tablespoons granulated sugar

3 eggs

1 tablespoon unsalted butter, melted

Utensils & Tools

Liquid measuring cup

Dry measuring cups

Measuring spoons

Large mixing bowl

Wire whisk

Crepe pan or medium-size frying pan

Pastry brush

Spatula

Cook on the
Stove

Get Cooking!

1. In a large mixing bowl, combine the flour and salt and make a well in the center.

2. Add 1⅓ cups of the milk and the sugar, and gently whisk together.

3. Add eggs, whisking until just blended.

4. Whisk in the remaining 1 cup of milk. Cover with plastic wrap and refrigerate for 30 minutes.

5. Heat crepe pan or frying pan over medium-high heat.

6. Brush the bottom and sides of the pan with melted butter.

7. Using a ¼-cup measure, pour the batter into the center of the pan. Quickly shake pan from side to side until batter evenly coats the bottom.

8. Cook until the underside is golden and the edges are starting to curl. Gently flip over and cook the other side until golden brown.

9. Remove the crepe from the pan with a spatula.

10. Repeat process with remaining melted butter and batter until all crepes are made.

Get creative! Serve with sliced fresh fruits, sweet butter, preserves, powdered sugar, sour cream or melted chocolate.

Get Ready, Get Set...

SERVINGS?
6-8

HOW MUCH TIME?

HOW DIFFICULT?

GUESS WHAT?
If you don't like bell peppers, you can substitute mushrooms or fresh tomatoes.

Cook on the **Stove**

Cook in the **Oven**

Ingredients

1 pound ground beef

1 package (8 ounces) refrigerated crescent rolls

1½ cups frozen hash brown potatoes, thawed

1½ cups shredded cheddar cheese

¼ cup finely chopped green bell pepper

5 eggs

⅓ cup milk

½ teaspoon salt

¼ teaspoon pepper

¼ cup grated Parmesan cheese

Pinch of dried oregano

Pinch of dried basil

Vegetable cooking spray

Utensils & Tools

Liquid measuring cup

Dry measuring cups

Measuring spoons

Large frying pan

Slotted spoon

Paper towels

12-inch round pizza pan

Small mixing bowl

Wire whisk

Get Cooking!

1. Preheat oven to 375°.

2. In a large frying pan over medium heat, cook beef until browned and crumbled.

3. Using a slotted spoon, remove the beef from the pan and drain on paper towels. Set aside.

4. On a sprayed 12-inch round pizza pan, form a pizza crust with the crescent dough.

5. Spread the beef evenly over the dough.

6. Sprinkle the hash browns and cheddar cheese over the beef.

7. In a small bowl, whisk together the eggs, milk, salt and pepper until frothy. Stir in the bell peppers.

8. Pour the egg mixture over the pizza crust.

9. Bake on the middle rack of the oven for 25 minutes or until the crust is golden brown and the filling has set.

10. Remove the pan from the oven using pot holders and sprinkle the top of the pizza with Parmesan cheese, oregano and basil.

11. Return the pan to the oven for an additional 5 minutes or until the cheese has melted.

12. Remove the pan from the oven using pot holders and cool slightly before serving.

Get Ready, Get Set...

MAKES
8 pancakes

HOW MUCH TIME?

HOW DIFFICULT?

GUESS WHAT?

♥ Why is this good for you? These pancakes provide a hearty breakfast that will fuel your morning. Rich in vitamins, minerals and fiber—you will feel the difference.

Cook on the
Stove

Ingredients

½ cup whole-wheat flour

½ cup unbleached all-purpose flour

1 tablespoon granulated sugar

1 teaspoon baking powder

1 teaspoon cinnamon

1 egg

1 cup nonfat milk

½ teaspoon vanilla extract

1 tablespoon vegetable oil

2 tablespoons orange juice

½ cup fresh blueberries or
    ½ cup frozen blueberries, thawed

Maple syrup or applesauce

Vegetable cooking spray

Utensils & Tools

Liquid measuring cup

Dry measuring cups

Measuring spoons

Large mixing bowl

Wire whisk

Small mixing bowl

Wooden spoon

Medium-size frying pan

Spatula

Get Cooking!

1. In a large mixing bowl, whisk together the flours, sugar, baking powder and cinnamon (dry ingredients). Form a well in the middle. Set aside.

2. In a small mixing bowl, whisk the egg until foamy.

3. Add the milk, vanilla extract and oil, and mix to combine.

4. Gently pour the liquid mixture into the well of the dry ingredients and mix until just blended.

5. Add the orange juice and mix to combine.

6. Gently stir in the blueberries.

7. Using a ¼-cup measure, pour the batter into the center of a lightly sprayed medium-size frying pan.

8. Cook for approximately 3 minutes or until underside becomes golden brown.

9. Using a spatula, flip pancake over and continue to cook until other side is golden brown.

10. Remove from the pan with a spatula and repeat with remaining butter.

Serve with a drizzle of maple syrup or applesauce.

BRUNCH IS BREAKFAST PLUS LUNCH.

Lunch plus supper is Lupper, but that's another chapter, another book. When adults go to brunch, it's all about coffee and talking. Our brunches rule...meals that are square, fun to prepare, eat anywhere...you won't want to share! But if you don't share, you don't get dessert for your tummy. Dessert plus tummy is...well, nevermind.

BRUNCH, LUNCH & MUNCH

Tuna Meltdowns 94

Rockin' Roll-Ups 96

Bow-Tie Pasta Salad 98

Biscuit-Bite Pizza 100

Tasty Tart 102

Chicken Veggie Sticks 104

♥ Gobble-Em-Up Turkey Burgers 106

Get Ready, Get Set...

SERVINGS?
6

HOW MUCH TIME?

HOW DIFFICULT?

GUESS WHAT?
If you want to add a little more zip to your tuna, add some pickle relish or diced celery.

Ingredients

2 cans (6 ounces each) of tuna packed in water

1 tablespoon mayonnaise

6 English muffins

1½ cups shredded cheddar cheese

Utensils & Tools

Measuring spoons

Dry measuring cups

Medium mixing bowl

Baking sheet

Cook in the
Oven

Get Cooking!

1. Preheat oven to 350°.

2. In a medium mixing bowl, mix together the tuna fish and mayonnaise.

3. Equally distribute the tuna fish among the 6 English muffins.

4. Equally distribute the shredded cheddar cheese on top of each muffin.

5. Place the muffins on a baking sheet.

6. Bake on the middle rack of the oven for 10–15 minutes or until the cheese is completely melted.

7. Remove from the oven using pot holders and serve while warm.

ROCKIN' ROLL-UPS

Get Ready,
Get Set...

SERVINGS?
8

HOW MUCH TIME?

HOW DIFFICULT?

GUESS WHAT?
For a vegetarian variation, make asparagus roll-ups: Substitute 1 teaspoon lemon pepper for the Dijon mustard and asparagus spears for the ham.

Ingredients

1 package (8 ounces) of cream cheese, at room temperature

1 tablespoon honey Dijon mustard

1 cup (2 sticks) unsalted butter

8 slices of white bread

3/4 pound thinly sliced ham

1 cup grated Parmesan cheese

Vegetable cooking spray

Utensils & Tools

Dry measuring cups

Measuring spoons

2 small mixing bowls

Rolling pin

Baking sheet

Cook in the
Oven

Get Cooking!

1. Preheat oven to 300°.

2. In a small mixing bowl, combine the cream cheese with honey Dijon mustard. Set aside.

3. Melt the butter in the microwave or in a small saucepan on the stove. Transfer melted butter to a small mixing bowl.

4. Slice crusts off the bread.

5. Using a rolling pin, roll each piece of bread very thin.

6. Evenly spread cream cheese mixture on each slice of bread.

7. Place a thin slice of ham on each piece of bread and roll up lengthwise.

8. Dip the roll into melted butter.

9. Sprinkle the roll with Parmesan cheese.

10. Place rolls 1 inch apart on a lightly sprayed baking sheet.

11. Bake on the middle rack of the oven for 10–15 minutes or until lightly golden.

12. Remove from the oven with pot holders and let cool slightly before serving.

BOW-TIE PASTA SALAD

Get Ready, Get Set...

SERVINGS?
8-10

HOW MUCH TIME?

HOW DIFFICULT?

GUESS WHAT?
To make the cooked pasta ahead of time, toss the cooled pasta with the ¼ cup of olive oil and refrigerate until ready to use.

Cook on the
Stove

Ingredients

1 package (1 pound) farfalle (bow-tie) pasta

2 cups cherry tomatoes, cut in half

16 ounces (2 cups) mozzarella cheese, cut into ½-inch cubes

2 jars (about 1½ cups) marinated artichoke hearts, drained and cut into small pieces

¼ cup chopped fresh basil

¼ cup olive oil

3 tablespoons red wine vinegar

Pinch of salt, pinch of pepper

Utensils & Tools

Dry measuring cups

Measuring spoons

Large pot

Large mixing bowl

Colander

Get Cooking!

1. Bring a large pot of water to a boil and cook the pasta according to the package instructions.

2. In a large mixing bowl, combine the tomatoes, mozzarella, artichoke hearts, basil, olive oil and vinegar.

3. When the pasta is cooked, drain in a colander. Immediately run cold water over the pasta for 1 minute. Drain again.

4. Add the pasta to the mixing bowl and mix all ingredients together.

5. Add salt and pepper.

Serve in individual bowls.

BISCUIT-BITE PIZZA

Get Ready, Get Set...

MAKES
8 pizzas

HOW MUCH TIME?

HOW DIFFICULT?

GUESS WHAT?
Be careful—even if the outsides of the pizzas are cool, the insides remain hot! Don't burn yourself!

Ingredients

2 packages refrigerated biscuit dough (8 per package)

$\frac{1}{2}$ cup tomato sauce

$\frac{1}{2}$ cup shredded mozzarella cheese

$\frac{1}{2}$ cup shredded cheddar cheese

Oregano

Utensils & Tools

Liquid measuring cup

Dry measuring cups

Baking sheet

Pastry brush

Cook in the
Oven

Get Cooking!

1. Preheat oven to 350°.

2. Using your hands, flatten each biscuit.

3. Place 8 flattened biscuits on a baking sheet, 1 inch apart.

4. Place 1 tablespoon of sauce, 1 tablespoon of each cheese and a small pinch of oregano on top of each biscuit.

5. Using the remaining 8 flattened biscuits, cover the topped biscuits.

6. Use a fork to seal the edges of the two layers.

7. Bake on the middle rack of the oven for 10 minutes or until golden brown.

8. Remove baking sheet from the oven with pot holders and set aside to cool slightly before eating.

TASTY TART

Get Ready, Get Set...

SERVINGS?
8

HOW MUCH TIME?

HOW DIFFICULT?

GUESS WHAT?
Readymade pie dough from the grocery store may be substituted for the homemade tart dough (and reduces difficulty too).

Cook on the
Stove

Cook in the
Oven

Ingredients

For the tart dough

1 cup all-purpose flour, placed in a small bowl in the freezer for 1 hour

1½ teaspoons salt

4 tablespoons (½ stick) unsalted butter, chilled and cut into small pieces

2 tablespoons vegetable shortening, chilled and cut into small pieces

2–3 tablespoons ice water

For the filling

½ pound (8 slices) bacon, chopped

2 cups shredded Swiss cheese

1 yellow onion, finely chopped

4 medium-size Yukon gold potatoes, sliced thin

2 tablespoons unsalted butter, melted

Pinch of salt, pinch of pepper

Utensils & Tools

Dry measuring cups	Medium-size frying pan
Measuring spoons	Plastic wrap
Small mixing bowl	Slotted spoon
Medium mixing bowl	Paper towels
Wire whisk	Rolling pin
Two dull knives	Baking sheet

Get Cooking!

1. In a medium mixing bowl, whisk together the flour and salt. Add the butter and shortening. Cut the butter and shortening into the flour using two dull knives or your hands, until mixture resembles small peas. Slowly add ice water and continue to mix just until dough comes together.

2. Form finished dough into the shape of a disk. Cover with plastic wrap and refrigerate at least 30 minutes.

3. In a medium-size frying pan over medium-high heat, add the bacon pieces and cook until nicely browned. Remove pieces from the pan with a slotted spoon and drain on paper towels.

4. Add the onions and cook for 3–4 minutes. Remove with a slotted spoon and drain on paper towels.

5. Preheat oven to 375°.

6. Place dough on a lightly floured surface. Roll into a circle about ¼ inch thick. Put on a baking sheet.

7. In a small mixing bowl, mix together the bacon, cheese and onions.

8. Spread the bacon, cheese and onion mixture on top of the dough, leaving a 2-inch border.

9. Layer the top of the tart with the potato slices, slightly overlapping each them.

10. Brush the tops of the potatoes with melted butter. Sprinkle with salt and pepper.

11. Fold the edges of the tart dough up to the outer layer of potatoes to make a crust.

12. Bake on the middle rack of the oven for 25 minutes or until the crust is golden brown.

13. Remove from the oven using pot holders, cut into 8 equal wedges and serve warm.

CHICKEN VEGGIE STICKS

Get Ready, Get Set...

SERVINGS?
6

HOW MUCH TIME?

HOW DIFFICULT?

GUESS WHAT?
These sticks taste great served over white rice with soy sauce.

Ingredients

3 chicken breasts, boneless and skinless

3 small zucchini

12 button mushrooms

12 cherry tomatoes

Utensils & Tools

6 wooden or metal skewers

Baking sheet

Cook in the
Oven

Get Cooking!

1. Preheat oven to 350°.

2. Cut each chicken breast into 6 equal pieces.

3. Cut the zucchini into thick round slices.

4. On each skewer alternately place 3 pieces of chicken, 2 mushrooms and 2 cherry tomatoes.

5. Repeat this process 5 times, until all skewers have been filled.

6. Place kebabs on a baking sheet.

7. Bake on the middle rack of the oven for 15–20 minutes or until the chicken is white and soft.

8. Remove from the oven using pot holders and serve while warm.

Get Ready, Get Set...

MAKES
4 burgers

HOW MUCH TIME?

HOW DIFFICULT?

GUESS WHAT?

♥ *Why is this good for you?*
A great alternative to hamburger, turkey breast is high in protein and low in fat. It is also a good source of B vitamins, iron and zinc.

Ingredients

1 pound ground turkey breast meat
1 teaspoon low-sodium soy sauce
2 teaspoons honey Dijon mustard
¼ cup finely chopped onion
4 whole-grain buns
Assorted burger toppings
Vegetable cooking spray

Utensils & Tools

Dry measuring cups
Measuring spoons
Large mixing bowl
Baking sheet
Spatula

Cook in the
Oven

Get Cooking!

1. Preheat oven broiler to medium heat.

2. In a large mixing bowl, mix together the ground turkey, soy sauce, mustard and onion.

3. Shape the meat mixture into 4 patties and place on a lightly sprayed baking sheet.

4. Broil in the oven for approximately 4–5 minutes or until the tops are well browned.

5. Remove from the oven using pot holders and flip burgers over with a spatula.

6. Return the sheet to the oven and cook for an additional 4–5 minutes or until the other side is well browned.

7. Remove from the oven using pot holders and serve warm.

Serve on whole-grain buns with lettuce, tomato or any of your favorite toppings.

Variation:

For cheeseburgers, add slices of your favorite cheese to the burgers 30 seconds before removing them from the oven.

WHETHER YOUR BIRTHDAY PARTY is small and special or big and loud, here are all kinds of fun food ideas you can try any time at all. It doesn't even have to be your birthday! You can celebrate with Fundue for your cat's birthday, or make the Peachy-Keen Cake to celebrate your dentist's. And remember, someone at your school must be a year older today...So take a deep breath and blow up a balloon. The fun will be in the cooking!

BIRTHDAY SURPRISES

Peachy-Keen Cake 114

Angel Fruit Cake 116

Fundue 118

Teatime with Scones 120

Brownie Sundaes 122

Favorite Chocolate Cake 124

❤ Cheesy Strawberry Cake 126

PEACHY-KEEN CAKE

Get Ready, Get Set...

SERVINGS?
10–12

HOW MUCH TIME?

HOW DIFFICULT?

GUESS WHAT?
It is important not to overmix the cake batter once the dry ingredients are added or the cake will have a tough texture.

Cook in the
Oven

Ingredients

For the peaches

6 peaches, peeled and sliced

8 tablespoons (1 stick) unsalted butter

1 cup granulated sugar

For the cake batter

1¾ cups all-purpose flour

2 teaspoons baking powder

½ teaspoon baking soda

2 teaspoons ground ginger

½ teaspoon ground cloves

¼ teaspoon ground nutmeg

1 teaspoon salt

10 tablespoons (5 ounces) unsalted butter

1 cup dark brown sugar

2 eggs

1 teaspoon vanilla extract

1 cup buttermilk

Flour for dusting

Vegetable cooking spray

Utensils & Tools

Liquid measuring cup

Dry measuring cups

Measuring spoons

10-inch round cake pan

Large frying pan

Medium mixing bowl

Large mixing bowl

Electric mixer

Wooden spoon

Wire rack

Get Cooking!

1. Preheat oven to 350°.

2. Lightly spray and flour a 10-inch round cake pan. Set aside.

3. In a large frying pan, melt 8 tablespoons of butter. Add the granulated sugar and cook until the sugar has melted and is a deep caramel brown color.

4. Add the peach slices to the pan and cook for 4–5 minutes.

5. Pour the peaches into the prepared cake pan and arrange nicely on the bottom of the pan. Set aside.

6. In a medium mixing bowl, sift together the flour, baking powder, baking soda, ginger, cloves, nutmeg and salt (dry ingredients). Set aside.

7. In a large mixing bowl, using an electric mixer, cream together the butter and brown sugar until light and fluffy. Add the buttermilk and beat on high speed for 2–3 minutes.

8. Using a wooden spoon, gently stir in the dry ingredients. Stir until just blended.

9. Pour batter over peaches in cake pan.

10. Bake on the middle rack of the oven for 30–35 minutes or until the top of the cake has completely set.

11. Remove the pan from the oven using pot holders and cool 10–15 minutes on a wire rack.

12. Turn pan upside down onto a serving plate and gently move pan away from cake.

Cut into slices and serve.

ANGEL FRUIT CAKE

Get Ready, Get Set...

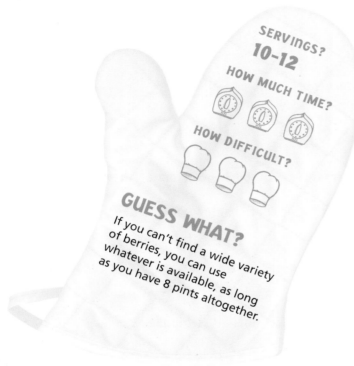

SERVINGS?
10-12

HOW MUCH TIME?

HOW DIFFICULT?

GUESS WHAT?
If you can't find a wide variety of berries, you can use whatever is available, as long as you have 8 pints altogether.

Cook in the
Oven

Ingredients

For the cake

16 egg whites

³/4 teaspoon cream of tartar

¹/4 teaspoon salt

1 teaspoon vanilla extract

2 tablespoons water

1¹/2 cups granulated sugar

¹/2 cup all-purpose flour

For the fruit topping

2 cups strawberries, washed and cut into quarters

2 cups raspberries

2 cups blackberries

2 cups blueberries

1 cup granulated sugar

¹/2 cup freshly squeezed lemon juice

Utensils & Tools

Liquid measuring cup

Dry measuring cups

Measuring spoons

Electric mixer

2 medium mixing bowls

Sifter or strainer

Tube pan (or large loaf pan)

Wire rack

Get Cooking!

1. Preheat oven to 375°.

2. Using an electric mixer on high speed, beat together the egg whites, cream of tartar, salt, vanilla and water for 10–12 minutes. With the mixer still on high speed, gradually add 1 cup of the sugar and beat until combined.

3. In a medium mixing bowl, sift together the flour and the remaining ½ cup of sugar. Pour over the beaten egg whites and gently mix until just blended.

4. Pour batter into a tube pan and bake on the middle rack of the oven for 30–35 minutes or until top begins to brown.

5. Remove from oven with pot holders and immediately turn upside down onto a wire rack.

6. Lift pan away from the cake and leave to cool for at least 1 hour.

7. While cake is cooling, combine all topping ingredients in a medium mixing bowl.

8. With the back side of a large spoon, slightly mash the ingredients together. Set aside the fruit topping for 30 minutes to allow the flavors to fully develop.

Serve the fruit topping spooned over the top of each slice of cake.

FUNDUE

Get Ready, Get Set...

SERVINGS?
6-8

HOW MUCH TIME?

HOW DIFFICULT?

GUESS WHAT?
Give your guests skewers for their dippers, so they don't get chocolate all over their fingers!

Cook on the
Stove

Ingredients

For the fundue

3/4 cup heavy cream

1/4 teaspoon salt

2 tablespoons light corn syrup

1 3/4 cups semi-sweet chocolate chips

2 1/2 teaspoons vanilla extract

For the dippers

Strawberries, washed and dried

Store-bought pound cake, cut into pieces

Bananas, cut into chunks

Utensils & Tools

Liquid measuring cup

Dry measuring cups

Measuring spoons

Medium saucepan

Wooden spoon

Serving bowl

Get Cooking!

1. In a medium saucepan over medium heat, bring the cream, salt and corn syrup to a boil.

2. Remove pan from the heat and add the chocolate chips all at once. Stir the chocolate until it has completely melted. If the chocolate does not completely melt, briefly return the pan to the stove on very low heat.

3. Stir in the vanilla extract and pour into a serving bowl.

Serve immediately with assorted fruits and pound cake, for dipping.

TEATIME WITH SCONES

Get Ready, Get Set...

MAKES
8 scones

HOW MUCH TIME?

HOW DIFFICULT?

GUESS WHAT?

Tea sandwiches are always present at teatime. At a traditional English tea, scones are served with sweet butter and jam.

Cook in the
Oven

Ingredients

3 cups all-purpose flour

1/3 cup granulated sugar

1 1/2 tablespoons baking powder

3/4 teaspoon baking soda

1 1/2 teaspoons salt

5 tablespoons unsalted butter, chilled and cut into small pieces

3 cups cream

1 cup currants (optional)

Cream for brushing

Granulated sugar for sprinkling

Utensils & Tools

Liquid measuring cup

Dry measuring cups

Measuring spoons

Large mixing bowl

Sifter or strainer

Two dull knives

Baking sheet

Pastry brush

Wire rack

Get Cooking!

Making Scones

1. Preheat oven to 400°.

2. In a large mixing bowl, sift the flour, sugar, baking powder, baking soda and salt (dry ingredients).

3. With two dull knives, cut the butter into the dry ingredients until the mixture resembles small peas.

4. Add the cream and mix well until dough is smooth, soft and slightly sticky. Stir in currants, if used, and distribute evenly.

5. Turn dough out onto a lightly floured work surface and knead briefly with your hands. Add enough flour so that the dough is not sticky.

6. Form dough into a circle, about 10 inches in diameter and 1 inch thick. Cut into 8 wedges.

7. Place scones on a baking sheet 1 inch apart. Brush the tops with cream and sprinkle with sugar.

8. Bake on the middle rack of the oven for 15–18 minutes or until golden brown.

9. Remove sheet from oven using pot holders and cool on a wire rack.

Making Tea

To brew a pot of tea, bring 4 cups of water to a boil, using either a kettle or a large pan. Pour the boiling water into a teapot with either 4 tea bags or ¼ cup of loose tea inside a tea ball. Let the pot sit for 4 minutes before serving.

Making Tea Sandwiches

To make tea sandwiches, cut the crusts off of your favorite sliced bread. Fill the sandwiches with such ingredients as cheese, ham, turkey or cucumber. Cut each sandwich into 4 triangles and serve.

BROWNIE SUNDAES

Get Ready, Get Set...

SERVINGS?
8-12

HOW MUCH TIME?

HOW DIFFICULT?

GUESS WHAT?

When cutting the brownies, make even rows of 3 across and 3 down, like a tic-tac-toe board, to equal 9 evenly cut brownies.

Ingredients

For the brownies

$\frac{1}{2}$ cup all-purpose flour

$\frac{1}{4}$ cup cocoa powder

$\frac{1}{2}$ teaspoon salt

$\frac{3}{4}$ cup semi-sweet chocolate chips

8 tablespoons (1 stick) unsalted butter, cut into small pieces

3 eggs

1 cup granulated sugar

1 teaspoon vanilla extract

Vanilla ice cream

Vegetable cooking spray

For the chocolate sauce

1 cup heavy cream

$1\frac{1}{2}$ cups semi-sweet chocolate chips

Utensils & Tools

Liquid measuring cup	Small saucepan
Dry measuring cups	Stainless steel bowl
Measuring spoons	Electric mixer
8-inch square cake pan	Wire whisk
2 medium mixing bowls	Wire rack
Sifter or strainer	Ice cream scoop

Cook on the
Stove

Cook in the
Oven

Get Cooking!

1. Preheat oven to 350°.

2. Lightly spray and flour an 8-inch square cake pan. Set aside.

3. In a medium mixing bowl, sift together the flour, cocoa powder and salt (dry ingredients). Set aside.

4. In a small saucepan, bring 1 cup of water to a boil. Place the chocolate chips and butter in a stainless steel bowl and set it on top of the saucepan. Turn the burner off and allow the chocolate to melt over the steaming water.

5. In another medium mixing bowl, using an electric mixer, whisk together eggs and sugar until pale yellow and slightly thickened. Stir in the vanilla extract. Slowly add the dry ingredients, mixing only until just blended.

6. Pour batter into prepared cake pan and bake on the middle rack of the oven for approximately 25 minutes or until a wooden skewer or toothpick poked in the middle of the cake comes out clean.

7. Remove from the oven using pot holders and cool pan on a wire rack before cutting.

8. In a small saucepan, bring cream just to a boil; remove from heat and pour over chocolate pieces. Whisk until all chocolate has melted.

9. To assemble the brownie sundae, scoop vanilla ice cream onto a brownie and drizzle chocolate sauce over the top.

FAVORITE CHOCOLATE CAKE

Get Ready, Get Set...

SERVINGS?
8-10

HOW MUCH TIME?

HOW DIFFICULT?

GUESS WHAT?
When adding the dry ingredients and buttermilk, beat only until just blended or the brownies will turn out hard and tough.

Cook in the
Oven

Ingredients

1½ cups cocoa powder

2 cups flour

½ teaspoon baking powder

1 teaspoon salt

12 ounces (3 sticks) unsalted butter, at room temperature

3 cups granulated sugar

2 teaspoons vanilla extract

6 eggs

1¼ cups buttermilk

1 cup semi-sweet chocolate chips

Vegetable cooking spray

Utensils & Tools

Liquid measuring cup

Dry measuring cups

Measuring spoons

10-inch tube pan

Medium mixing bowl

Sifter or strainer

Electric mixer

Spoon

Toothpick

Wire rack

Get Cooking!

1. Preheat oven to 350°.

2. Spray and flour a 10-inch tube pan.

3. In a medium mixing bowl, sift together the cocoa powder, flour, baking powder and salt (dry ingredients). Set aside.

4. Using an electric mixer on medium-high speed, cream together the butter and sugar until light and fluffy.

5. Add the vanilla. Add the eggs one at a time, beating at least 1 minute between each addition.

6. On low speed, add ⅓ of the dry ingredients, then ½ of the buttermilk, beating between each addition. Add another ⅓ of the dry ingredients, then the remaining ½ of the buttermilk, beating between each addition. Add the remaining dry ingredients.

7. With a spoon, gently stir in chocolate chips.

8. Pour the batter into prepared pan and bake on the middle rack of the oven for 45–55 minutes or until a toothpick poked in the middle of the cake comes out clean.

9. Remove pan from the oven using pot holders and set aside to cool for 20 minutes.

10. Turn pan upside down onto a wire rack and gently lift pan away from cake.

Cut into slices and serve.

CHEESY STRAWBERRY CAKE

Get Ready, Get Set...

SERVINGS?
8-10

HOW MUCH TIME?

HOW DIFFICULT?

GUESS WHAT?

♥ Why is this good for you? This delicious cheesecake is high in calcium and low in fat—enjoy this treat as a birthday alternative or at any time of the year!

Cook in the
Oven

Ingredients

For the crust

2–3 graham crackers
(enough to make ½ cup crumbs)

½ cup margarine, melted

2–4 tablespoons hot water

Vegetable cooking spray

For the filling

1 whole egg

2 egg whites

3 packages (8 ounces) nonfat cream cheese, at room temperature

½ cup granulated sugar

For the topping

2 cups (16 ounces) nonfat sour cream

3 tablespoons granulated sugar

2 cups strawberries, washed and sliced

Utensils & Tools

Liquid measuring cup

Dry measuring cups

Measuring spoons

10-inch springform pan

Food processor

Medium mixing bowl

2 small mixing bowls

Electric mixer

Toothpick

Wire whisk

Wire rack

Get Cooking!

1. Preheat oven to 350°.

2. Spray a 10-inch springform pan lightly with vegetable cooking spray.

3. Blend graham crackers in a food processor to make ½ cup crumbs.

4. In a medium mixing bowl, combine the melted margarine and the crumbs. Add a little hot water if the mixture is too dry.

5. Using your hands, spread and pat the mixture firmly into the bottom of the springform pan. Set aside.

6. In a small mixing bowl, whisk together the egg and egg whites. Set aside.

7. Using an electric mixer on medium-high speed, blend the cream cheese until smooth. Add the sugar and continue to blend. Add the eggs and blend until the mixture is smooth and creamy.

8. Pour the cream cheese mixture over the crust in the springform pan.

9. Bake on the middle rack of the oven for 30–35 minutes or until a toothpick poked into the center of the cake comes out dry and the cake pulls away from the sides of the pan.

10. Remove the cake from the oven using pot holders.

11. Increase oven temperature to 400°.

12. In a small mixing bowl, whisk together the sour cream and sugar. Evenly pour the mixture over the top of the cake. Return the pan to the oven for an additional 5 minutes.

13. Remove cake from the oven using pot holders and set on a wire rack to cool.

14. After the cake has cooled, place in refrigerator for 2–4 hours to set.

Serve with fresh strawberries.

INDEX WHAT'S IN THE KITCHEN?

BASICS

Most kitchens have on hand the following staples:
- salt and pepper
- flours, sugars and syrups
- milk and eggs
- butter and shortening
- olive oil and vegetable cooking spray
- vinegar, lemon juice and mayonnaise
- baking powder and baking soda
- vanilla extract and dried yeast
- lots of herbs and seasonings

These ingredients are not listed below, unless they are a main part of a recipe.

BEANS AND GRAINS

Beans, kidney..............38
Cereal nuggets..............26
Corn meal..............44
Popcorn..............14

BREADS, CHIPS AND CRACKERS

Bread..............20
   cinnamon raisin..............80
   crumbs..............40
   white..............96
   whole-wheat..............80
Buns, whole-grain..............106
Chips
   corn..............38
   tortilla..............64
English muffins..............94
Graham crackers..............16, 126
Pretzels..............62
Tortillas, corn..............58

CHEESES AND MILK PRODUCTS

Buttermilk..............36, 78, 114, 124
Cheese..............120
   cheddar..............38, 64, 84, 94, 100
   cream..............64, 74, 96, 126
   jack..............76
   mozzarella..............44, 98, 100
   Parmesan..............44, 84, 96
   Swiss..............102
Cream..............120
   heavy..............76, 118, 122
   sour..............58, 126

Ice cream, vanilla..............56, 122
Milk, evaporated..............62
Sherbet, fruit..............66
Yogurt, frozen..............56, 66

CHOCOLATE

Bar of plain..............16
Candies..............14
Chips, semi-sweet..............18, 22, 78, 118, 122, 124
Cocoa powder..............122, 124

CANDIES AND SWEETS

Candies, chocolate-coated..............14
Honey..............62
Jam/jelly
   fruit..............54
   orange..............46
Ice cream, vanilla..............56, 122
Marshmallows..............14
   cream..............16
Sherbet, fruit..............66
Yogurt, frozen..............56, 66

EGGS

Whole..............74, 76, 82, 84
Whites..............116, 126

FISH

Cod or halibut filets..............36
Tuna..............94

FRUITS AND FRUIT JUICES

Apple..............24, 62
   juice concentrate..............26
   sauce..............80, 86
Avocado..............58
Banana..............22, 26, 56, 62, 66, 80, 118
Berries..............66
Blackberries..............116
Blueberries..............26, 86, 116
Currants..............120
Lemon..............116
Orange juice..............86
Peach..............114
Raisins..............24, 62
Raspberries..............116
Strawberries..............116, 118, 126

MEATS

Bacon..............102
Beef, ground..............38, 40, 42, 84

Chili without beans..............64
Ham..............74, 96, 120
Pork, ground..............40

NUTS AND NUT BUTTERS

Almonds, slivered..............62
Mixed nuts..............80
Peanut butter..............54, 56, 62
Peanuts..............14, 22
Pecans..............24

PASTAS

Farfalle (bow-tie)..............98
Spaghetti..............40

PASTRIES

Crescent rolls..............24, 84
Dough
   biscuit..............100
   pie..............34, 42
Pound cake..............54, 118

POULTRY

Chicken..............34
   breasts..............46, 104
Turkey..............120
   breast, ground..............106

SAUCES, DRESSINGS AND SOUPS

Mushroom soup, cream of..............34
Salad dressing..............38
Salsa..............58, 76
Tartar sauce..............36
Tomato sauce..............44, 100

VEGETABLES

Artichoke hearts, marinated..............98
Bell pepper, green..............84
Celery..............62
Carrots..............34, 42, 62
Corn..............34, 76
Cucumber..............120
Lettuce, head..............38
Mushrooms, button..............42, 104
Onion..............34, 40, 42, 64, 102, 106
Peas..............34
Potatoes
   hash brown..............84
   russet or Idaho..............36, 42
   Yukon gold..............102
Tomatoes..............38, 40
   cherry..............98, 104
Zucchini..............104